WOOD

A TRUE BOOK

by
Christin Ditchfield

Children's Press®
A Division of Scholastic Inc.

New York Toronto London Auckland Sydney
Mexico City New Delhi Hong Kong
Danbury, Connecticut

A young girl cuts a piece of wood for a project.

Content Consultant
Jan Jenner, Ph.D.

Reading Consultant
Nanci R. Vargus, Ed.D.
Primary Multiage Schools,
Indianapolis, IN

Library of Congress Cataloging-in-Publication Data

Ditchfield, Christin.
    Wood / by Christin Ditchfield.
        p.   cm.—(A true book)
    Includes bibliographical references and index.
    Summary: Describes different types of wood, where various kinds of
trees grow, and how wood is processed and used.
    ISBN 0-516-22346-1 (lib. bdg.)   0-516-29370-2 (pbk.)
    1. Wood—Juvenile literature. [1. Wood. 2. Trees.] I. Title. II. Series.
TA419 .D498 2002
620.1'2—dc21

                                                                    2001003569

CHILDREN'S PRESS, AND A TRUE BOOK®, and associated logos are
trademarks and or registered trademarks of Grolier Publishing Co., Inc.
SCHOLASTIC and associated logos are trademarks and or registered
trademarks of Scholastic Inc.

1 2 3 4 5 6 7 8 9 10 R 11 10 09 08 07 06 05 04 03 02

Contents

Who Needs Wood? 5

Where Is Wood Found? 10

What Is Wood Made of? 22

How Is Wood Processed? 28

What Is Next? 36

To Find Out More 44

Important Words 46

Index 47

Meet the Author 48

Have you ever thought about how important trees are?

Who Needs Wood?

Trees grow all around you. You see them every day. You may not think much about them, but trees give you one of the most valuable natural resources—wood. A natural resource is a substance found in nature that has many important uses. Wood is a strong, solid material that

Wood can provide heat and shelter.

can be cut and carved into many different shapes and sizes.

From the beginning of time, people have burned wood to provide warmth for their homes and heat for cooking. Houses and furniture are built with wood. Because it floats, wood can be used to make sturdy boats, ranging from one-person canoes to great sailing ships. There are wooden tools, wooden boxes, barrels, and bowls. Musical instruments, such as drums and violins, are made

Wood is used to make parts of many musical instruments, including drums and violins.

out of wood. Children play with toys made from wood, such as puzzles, dolls, baseball bats, and building blocks.

Many useful chemicals, such as rosin, turpentine, and tar, come from wood. Wood contains a fiber called cellulose that is used to make everything from toilet paper to camera film. The pencils you write with are made from wood, and the paper you write on comes from wood pulp.

You probably use a wooden pencil and paper made from wood in class every day.

One way or another, people use wood every single day!

Where Is Wood Found?

The wood that people use each day comes from trees. A place where many trees grow close together is called a forest. Scientists tell us that there are four major types of forests. There are deciduous forests, coniferous forests, tropical rain forests, and temperate rain forests. In each

The leaves on the trees of this deciduous forest in Vermont change color during the fall season.

of these forests, we find different kinds of trees.

The best known forest is the deciduous forest. **Deciduous** trees have flat, broad leaves. In the fall, these leaves change

Maple and elm trees can be found in deciduous forests.

color and fall off of the trees.
New leaves grow back in the
spring. Deciduous forests can
be found all over North
America, Europe, and Australia.
Deciduous trees include
maples, oaks, elms, and beech
trees. The wood that comes
from these trees is sturdy and
lasts a long time. It is most
often used to build houses and
furniture.

A **coniferous** forest is made
up of trees called conifers.

You can tell if a tree is a conifer by its spiked leaves called needles and its cones.

Conifers have cones and spiked leaves that look like needles. Because they stay green all year long, these trees are often called **evergreens**. Coniferous trees grow best in colder climates. Coniferous forests are

This coniferous forest is located in Alberta, Canada.
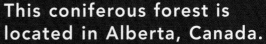

usually located in the northern parts of the world, in countries such as Canada and Russia. Conifers include fir trees, pine trees, cedars, and spruces. This wood is softer. Its **pulp** is used to make paper products.

Tropical rain forests look like hot, swampy jungles. The temperature in the forest stays at about 80° Fahrenheit (27° Celsius) all the time. Rain falls almost daily. A rain forest may receive as much as 150 inches (381 centimeters) of rain each year. Often, the forest is completely flooded. Because of the constant moisture in the air, the trees stay green throughout the year. In a tropical rain forest you will find mahogany, ebony, and teak trees. These trees take hundreds

Tropical rain forests (above) are very warm and receive a lot of rain. A man carves a figure out of a piece of mahogany wood (right).

of years to grow. The wood is extremely hard and very expensive. It is used to make decorative furniture and carved ornaments.

A temperate rain forest (above) gets a lot of rain, but is much cooler than a tropical rain forest. This giant redwood (right) is located in Sequoia National Park

Just like tropical rain forests, temperate rain forests are always wet. However, the weather is much cooler. These cold and foggy forests can be found along the coast in the Pacific Northwest, from California all the way to Alaska. Some of the oldest and tallest trees in the world grow there. Giant redwoods have measured more than 300 feet (90 meters) tall. Scientists say that some of the trees are more than four thousand years old! These trees are mostly coniferous evergreens, like Douglas firs, Sitka spruce, western spruce, and sequoias.

Check It Out!

You can grow your own tree in a paper cup!
You will need:

Tree seeds (seeds from
an apple or orange
work well)

Soil

Plastic bag with
a twist tie

Water

Paper cup

1. Poke a tiny draining hole in the bottom of a paper cup.

2. Fill the cup half-full of soil. Water the soil until it is very damp. Add a few seeds. Cover them with the remaining soil.

3. Place the cup inside a plastic bag and seal the bag with a twist tie. (The bag keeps moisture inside.) Set the cup in a warm place. Each day, open the bag and add water to the soil.

4. When you see the shoots coming up out of the dirt, gradually open the plastic bag a little at a time. As the tree grows, you can transfer it to a bigger pot or plant it outside.

What Is Wood Made of?

There are thousands of varieties of trees in the world. Different trees give us different types of wood. Some wood appears white or yellow. Some wood is dark brown. Other woods have a rich red color. If you could look deep inside a tree trunk, you would see that wood is

Fibers in the wood provide trees with their nourishment. They also carry fluids down from leaves to roots.

made of many little tubes. These tubes carry water and other **nutrients** from the roots of the tree all the way to the leaves. The tiny tubes are also called fibers.

Wood can be either open-grained (top) or closed-grained (bottom).

Wood fibers form a pattern called the **grain**. If the lines of the grain are wide and far apart, the wood is described as open-grained. When the lines of the grain are close together, the wood is close-grained.

Although all wood is hard, some woods are harder— more solid—than others. Most woods can be divided into either softwoods or hardwoods.

Softwoods are used to make many things, including musical instruments.

Softwoods include cedar, cypress, spruce, and pine. People use these open-grained woods for paper products, musical instruments, buildings, and ordinary everyday furniture.

Hardwoods include oak, walnut, mahogany, and teak. These close-grained woods can be used in shipbuilding, paneling, and cabinetmaking. Hardwoods are often made into expensive furniture and decorations.

Hardwoods are used to make boats, furniture, and lots of other items.

How Is Wood Processed?

To use wood, we have to process it. Some trees are harvested from natural forests. Others have been grown especially for wood production on tree farms called nurseries. Loggers use chain saws to cut down the trees and remove their leaves and branches.

Powerful saws are used
to cut down trees.

The cut trees are loaded onto trucks, which take the logs to a sawmill.

The logs are then loaded onto trucks or floated down the river to transport them to a sawmill.

At the sawmill, special machines remove all the tree bark. Other machines slice the wood into long, even pieces so that it can be used for building.

The logs go through a machine called a debarker that removes the bark from the log.

Freshly cut lumber is placed outside to dry.

This wood is called **lumber** or timber. Freshly cut lumber is wet because it still has tree sap in it. Workers stack piles of lumber out in the open air, where the wood can dry out.

The time it takes for the wood to dry is called seasoning. Seasoning may be a period of a few days or many months, depending on the kind of wood. When the wood has dried out, it will be shipped to factories and stores where it can be shaped into the things we use each day.

If the wood is to be used for paper, it must go through one more process. At a paper mill, workers feed pieces of lumber

To make paper, wood is first cut down into small wood chips, then water and chemicals are added to pulp, and finally the pulp is pressed into long flat layers that become paper.

into a machine called a shredder, which grinds them into little pieces. These wood chips are mixed with chemicals and heated, until they form a wet, mushy material called **pulp**. Iron rollers squeeze out the water and press the pulp into long, flat layers. The pressure of the rollers causes the pulp fibers to join tightly together. When it has dried completely, the pulp turns to paper. Workers wind the paper onto giant reels so that it can be transported to factories.

What Is Next?

Wood is an important part of everyday life. Unfortunately, people have not always taken good care of this precious resource. People have used the wood, but they have not cared for the trees that provide the wood. For many years, loggers chopped down thousands of

These two photographs show areas where trees were cut down without being replaced.

trees without replanting new ones. This harmed the environment and destroyed animal habitats. It even affected the weather. Areas where too many trees had been cut soon became deserts.

People who are careless with matches have started forest fires that destroyed acres and

Forest fires pose a threat to this important natural resource.

acres of valuable trees. Some factories have released danger-ous chemicals into our air, water, and soil. This pollution damages and even kills trees. Everyone uses **disposable** paper products on a regular basis. As you have learned, these products come from trees. In the United States alone, people throw away more than 70 to 80 million tons of paper each year! Only about 48 percent of this paper is recycled. That is a lot of wasted trees.

Recycling newspapers and other paper products will help save trees.

Reusing and recycling paper are two of the most important things you can do to save the trees. Recently, neighborhoods and communities have begun special programs to replace

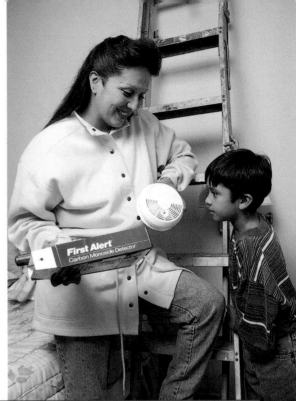

Planting trees and learning about fire safety are
two ways you can preserve this natural resource.

trees that have been cut
down. New trees are planted
to celebrate special occasions
and on national holidays, such
as Arbor Day. An arbor is a

place surrounded by trees. Some people have even adopted a tree. They water it, **prune** it, and care for it in the same way they would care for a flower in their garden. Schools teach children about fire safety and the dangers of playing with matches. Scientists have been trying to find ways to reduce pollution and protect our forests. If each person does his or her part, everyone will enjoy using wood for many years to come!

On the Job

When a tree gets sick, who do you call? A tree surgeon, of course! Tree surgeons are specially trained to care for trees. They cut off branches that are diseased. They build supports to hold up falling branches. Sometimes tree surgeons are called to remove trees that have been blown over by high winds in a storm. They help move trees from one place to another.

Tree surgeons usually work in teams of two. One person climbs up in the tree, while the other provides assistance from the ground. These tree doctors use a lot of heavy machinery, including chain saws, wood chippers, and stump grinders. To protect themselves from injury, tree surgeons wear special boots, gloves, and helmets.

To Find Out More

Here are some additional resources to help you learn more about wood:

 **Books**

Adams, Peter. **Early Loggers and the Sawmill.** Crabtree Publishing, 1999.

Chambers, Catherine. **Wood.** Raintree Steck-Vaughn Publishers, 1996.

Dyson, Sue. **Wood.** Thomson Learning, 1993.

Gamlin, Linda. **Eyewitness Explorers: Trees.** Dorling Kindersley, Ltd., 1997.

Hickman, Pamela. **In the Woods.** Formac Publishing Company, Ltd., 1998.

Kerrod, Robin. **Material Resources.** Thomson Learning, 1994.

Organizations and Online Sites

American Forestry Association
1516 P. St. NW
Washington, D.C. 20005

This conservation organization promotes proper management and appreciation of forests, soil, water, wildlife, and all other national resources.

American Forest & Paper Association
1111 19th Street NW,
Suite 800
Washington, D.C. 20036

This organization is the national trade association of the forest, paper, and wood products industry.

Planetpals Earthzone
http://www.planetpals.com

This online site provides facts and fun activities about Earth.

United States Department of Agriculture Forest Service
P.O. Box 96090
201 14th Street, SW
Washington, D.C. 20090
http://www.fs.fed.us/

"Caring for the Land and Serving People," this organization includes information on forestry, geology, conservation, and fire safety—as well as links to all of the National Forest websites.

United States Environmental Protection Agency Explorers' Club for Kids
http://www.epa.gov/kids/

This online site combines facts with fun—games, contests, and ways you can help protect the environment.

Important Words

coniferous an evergreen tree that produces cones

deciduous a tree that sheds its leaves every year

disposable something that is made to be thrown away after it is used

evergreen a bush or tree having leaves that stay green throughout the year

grain the pattern of tiny lines found on a piece of wood

lumber wood or timber that has been sawed

nutrient something needed by people, plants, and animals in order to stay healthy

prune to cut branches from a tree or bush, in order to help it grow stronger

pulp a soft, wet mixture made from wood

Index

(**Boldface** page numbers
indicate illustrations.)

Arbor Day, 41
cellulose, 8
chain saw, 28, **29,** 41
coniferous, 10, 13–15
debarker, **31**
deciduous, 10, **11,** 11–13
disposable, 39
evergreen, 14, 19
experiment, 20–21
fiber, 23, 25, 35
fire safety, **41,** 42
forest, 10
grain, **24,** 25
hardwood, 25, 27
lumber, 32–33, 35
musical instrument, 7, **7,**
  26
nursery, 28
nutrient, 23

paper mill, 33
pollution, 39, 42
prune, 42, 46
pulp, 15, 35
recycling, 40, **40**
redwood, 19
sawmill, 30–31
seasoning, 33
softwood, 25–26
temperate rain forest, 10,
  18–19
tree surgeon, 43
tropical rain forest, 10,
  16–17
wood
  hardwood, 25, 27
  processing, 28–35
  softwood, 25–26
  uses for, 5–9, 13, 15, 17
  what it's made of, 22–27
  where it's found, 10–21
wood chip, **34,** 35

Meet the Author

Christin Ditchfield is the author of a number of books for Children's Press, including five True Books on natural resources. A former elementary school teacher, she is now a freelance writer and conference speaker, and host of the nationally syndicated radio program, *Take It To Heart!* Ms. Ditchfield makes her home in Sarasota, Florida.